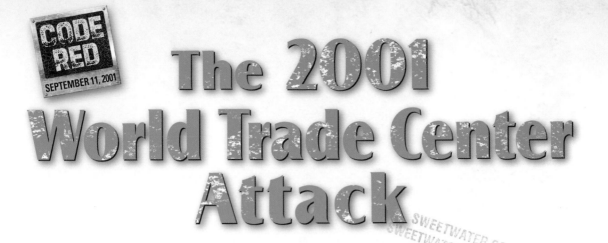

The 2001 World Trade Center Attack

by Jacqueline Dembar Greene

Consultant: Paul F. Johnston
Washington, D.C.

BEARPORT
PUBLISHING

New York, New York

Credits

Cover and Title Page, © Michelle V. Agins/The New York Times/Redux; 4–5, © AP Images/ Ed Bailey; 5, © REUTERS/Jeff Christensen; 6, © Masatomo Kuriya/Corbis; 8, © Justin Lane/ The New York Times/Redux; 9, © REUTERS/Shannon Stapleton; 10–11, © Jason Szenes/ CORBIS SYGMA; 12, Courtesy of The Office of the Deputy Commissioner, Public Information, NYPD; 13, © REUTERS/Shannon Stapleton; 14, © AP Images/Jim Collins; 15, © AP Images/Amy Sancetta; 16–17, © REUTERS/Ray Stubblebine; 18, © Justin Lane/ The New York Times/Redux; 19, © Bill Greenblatt/CORBIS SYGMA; 20, © Justin Lane/ The New York Times/Redux; 21, © REUTERS/Shaun Best; 22, © Bob Houlihan/U.S. Navy/ Getty Images/Newscom.com; 23, © AP Images; 24, © REUTERS/ Gerry Penny/POOL GP/ NMB/AA; 25, © REUTERS/Jim Hollander; 26–27, © Mark E. Gibson/CORBIS; 28T, Courtesy of Berkley Publishing Group, a division of Penguin Group, U.S.A.; 28B, © GuidingEyes.Org; 29T, © AP Images; 29B, © Darren McCollester/Getty Images/ Newscom.com; 29 Background, AbleStock/IndexOpen.

Publisher: Kenn Goin
Project Editor: Adam Siegel
Creative Director: Spencer Brinker
Photo Researcher: Marty Levick
Design: Dawn Beard Creative

Library of Congress Cataloging-in-Publication Data

Greene, Jacqueline Dembar.
  The 2001 World Trade Center attack / by Jacqueline Dembar Greene.
      p. cm. — (Code red)
  Includes bibliographical references and index.
  ISBN-13: 978-1-59716-365-1 (library binding)
  ISBN-10: 1-59716-365-1 (library binding)
  1. September 11 Terrorist Attacks, 2001—Juvenile
literature. 2. Fire fighters—New York State—New York—
Juvenile literature. 3. Heroes—United States—Juvenile
literature. I. Title.

  HV6432.7.G72 2007
  974.7'1044—dc22

                            2006030436

For more information, write to Bearport Publishing Company, Inc., 101 Fifth Avenue, Suite 6R, New York, New York 10003. Printed in the United States of America.

10 9 8 7 6 5 4 3 2 1

Contents

News of a Disaster

It was a sunny fall morning in New York City on
September 11, 2001. At 8:46 A.M., firefighters at the
station house of Ladder Company 6 heard a loud noise.
They looked up in surprise. A jet roared above them.
It was flying low—too low.

North
Tower

South
Tower

In another fire station about 100 blocks north, the **intercom** crackled on. A voice told the firefighters to turn on the television, quickly. Commander Richard Picciotto (*pich*-ee-OH-toh), or "Chief Pitch," watched the news, stunned.

"I saw what everyone else saw," he later remembered. "The North Tower of the World Trade Center, smoking like crazy." He could barely believe his eyes. A plane had crashed into the **skyscraper**.

Smoke poured from the North Tower. It had been struck between the 94th and 98th floors by American Airlines Flight 11.

The Twin Towers were made up of the North Tower and the South Tower. About 50,000 people worked in the Twin Towers. Each day 26,000 tourists visited the buildings.

Racing to the Rescue

Within minutes, a crew from Ladder Company 6 arrived at the scene. Chunks of **debris** were falling from the burning building.

The firefighters dashed inside the North Tower. Each of them was carrying gear that weighed about 60 pounds (27 kg). Suddenly, they felt a jolt. A second plane had just crashed into the South Tower of the World Trade Center. It was 9:03 A.M.

As people below watched in horror, United Airlines Flight 175 crashed between the 78th and 84th floors of the South Tower.

Chief Pitch saw the second plane crash on television. At once, he was on his way. He drove to the World Trade Center at full speed, with sirens blaring. There, he saw flames shooting from the top floors of both towers.

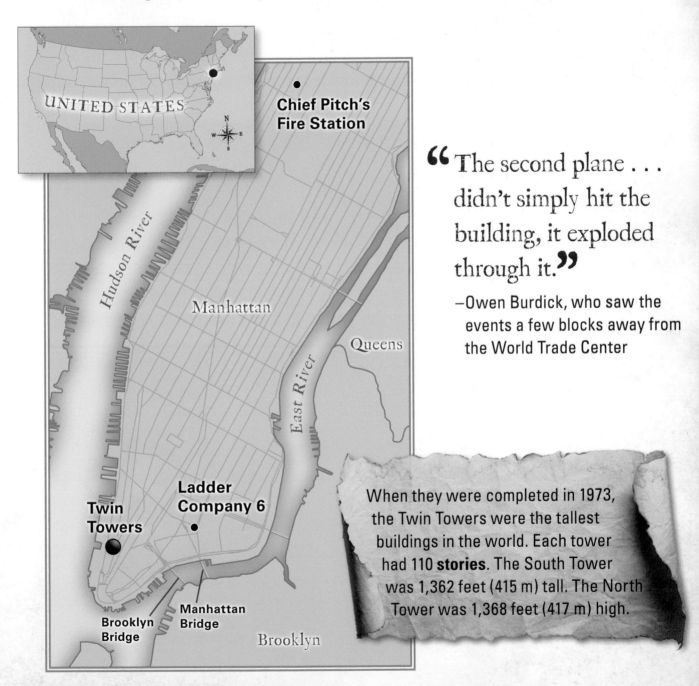

Chief Pitch's Fire Station

Manhattan

Queens

Ladder Company 6

Twin Towers

Manhattan Bridge

Brooklyn Bridge

Brooklyn

Hudson River

East River

UNITED STATES

66 The second plane . . . didn't simply hit the building, it exploded through it. 99

–Owen Burdick, who saw the events a few blocks away from the World Trade Center

When they were completed in 1973, the Twin Towers were the tallest buildings in the world. Each tower had 110 **stories**. The South Tower was 1,362 feet (415 m) tall. The North Tower was 1,368 feet (417 m) high.

The island of Manhattan makes up part of New York City, along with Brooklyn, Queens, Staten Island, and the Bronx.

7

A Long Way Down

Workers inside the World Trade Center knew they had to get out. Donna Enright worked on the 71st floor of the North Tower. She rushed to help her friend Omar Rivera, who was blind. His guide dog, Salty, helped him get to and from work every day.

Omar Rivera and his guide dog, Salty

Rivera, Enright, and Salty joined the crowd of escaping workers. They filed down the many flights of stairs as quickly as they could.

At the same time, hundreds of firefighters hurried up the stairs. They began to search the building for **survivors**. They found many empty offices. Computer screens flickered, and cups of coffee sat on deserted desks.

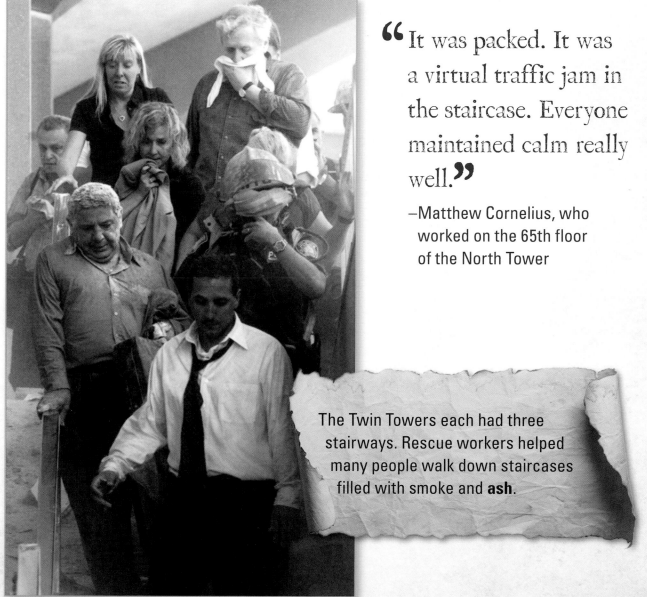

"It was packed. It was a virtual traffic jam in the staircase. Everyone maintained calm really well."

–Matthew Cornelius, who worked on the 65th floor of the North Tower

The Twin Towers each had three stairways. Rescue workers helped many people walk down staircases filled with smoke and **ash**.

Trapped

The two planes that hit the World Trade Center held about 20,000 gallons (75,708 l) of fuel. This jet fuel was very **flammable**. After the planes crashed into the buildings, the fuel erupted into smoky flames.

Debris and smoke from the enormous fires blocked the stairways. People on the upper floors had no way to escape.

James Gartenberg called his wife from the 86th floor of the North Tower. "I love you. . . . I don't know if I'm going to get out of it," he told her.

The Twin Towers' sprinkler systems could not put out the fierce blazes. As the smoke and fire rose higher, people began to jump from the burning buildings.

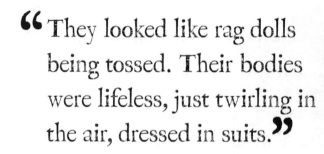

" They looked like rag dolls being tossed. Their bodies were lifeless, just twirling in the air, dressed in suits. "

–Edgardo Villagas, who worked in the World Trade Center, describing people jumping

Clouds of black smoke poured from the World Trade Center as the jet fuel burned. People could see the smoke from as far away as New Jersey and Connecticut.

11

Like a War Zone

Thousands of people made it down the towers. Police officers hurried them out of the buildings. "Don't look," shouted Officer Moira Smith. "Keep moving!" She waved her flashlight to point the way out.

One man later said Officer Smith saved many lives. He could see the officer was scared, but she never lost courage.

New York Police Department officer Moira Smith

> **"Heroism is not only running into flames. It is doing your job in the face of horror."**
>
> –Martin Glynn, remembering how Officer Smith saved his life and hundreds of others

Twenty-three officers from the New York City Police Department died on September 11. Officer Moira Smith was the only woman among them.

The survivors were not yet safe, however. Some described the area outside the towers as a war zone. On the ground lay dead bodies. Pieces of concrete and broken glass covered everything.

Ash filled the air and made it difficult to see. People held cloths over their noses and mouths to help them breathe.

The South Tower Falls

The heat of the fires had damaged the South Tower's steel support beams. They were no longer strong enough to hold the building up. At 9:59 A.M., only 56 minutes after it was hit, the building **collapsed**.

> **"**I'm four blocks north of the World Trade Center. The [South Tower] . . . has just completely collapsed. It folded down on itself, and it is not there anymore.**"**
>
> –Don Dahler,
> television reporter

The South Tower fell in a blast of smoke, cement, steel, and glass.

Enormous clouds of dust and ash rose into the air. The gray and white powder covered the surrounding area. One survivor recalled, "The dust cloud was ten stories high and came down the street for blocks faster than it could be outrun."

Some people had gathered in nearby Trinity Church. They heard the huge explosion as the tower fell. They saw "tons of debris" blowing toward them. The sunny sky now looked black.

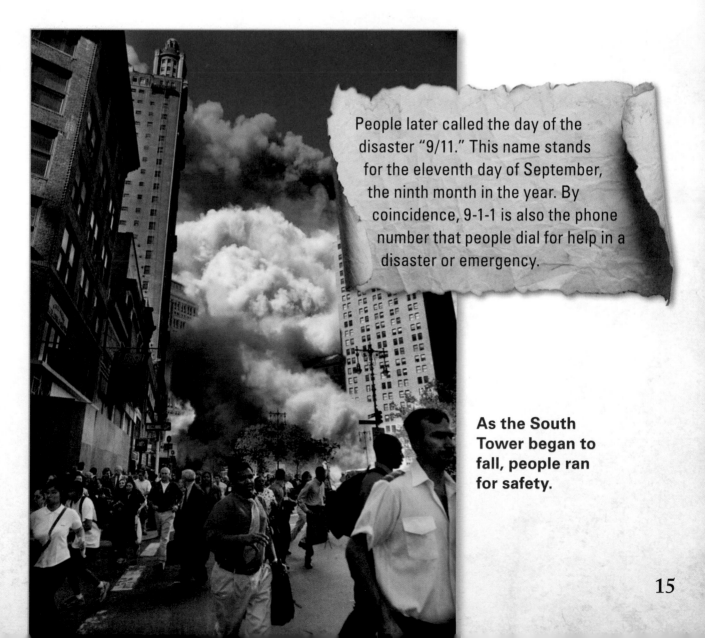

People later called the day of the disaster "9/11." This name stands for the eleventh day of September, the ninth month in the year. By coincidence, 9-1-1 is also the phone number that people dial for help in a disaster or emergency.

As the South Tower began to fall, people ran for safety.

The North Tower Falls

People in the North Tower were now in great danger. It, too, could fall at any minute.

Chief Pitch was on the 35th floor. He sent a radio message to all the rescue workers in the building. "Get out! Drop your masks! Drop your tools! Drop everything! This is an **evacuation**!" he yelled.

More than 1,000 people were still inside the North Tower when it collapsed.

Everyone had to get out of the building. Rescue workers helped those who could not walk alone.

They did not have much time. At 10:28 A.M., the North Tower collapsed. A second shower of dust and ash blanketed the area. It was less than half an hour after the South Tower had fallen.

Three hundred and forty-three firefighters died trying to save others on September 11.

17

A City of Heroes

The survivors were in shock. People on the streets could barely see through the thick dust. Many were injured, bleeding, or burned. Emergency workers did all they could. They rushed people to hospitals.

Many ordinary people acted like heroes. Strangers helped one another. Store owners gave bottles of water to dusty survivors.

Firefighters and emergency workers gave injured people first aid on the street.

After the disaster, Manhattan shut down. Subway trains stopped running. Cars were not allowed to drive onto or off the island. Many people had to walk over bridges to get home. Roselyn Braud had escaped from the basement of the World Trade Center. Now she could barely walk. Two strangers supported her across the Manhattan Bridge.

After the disaster, New York and other states asked citizens to help the injured by giving blood. Thousands of Americans donated blood in the following weeks.

Ground Zero

The place where the Twin Towers once stood was now a mountain of burning **rubble**. Rescue workers began searching for survivors at **Ground Zero** right away.

Firefighters rescued Chief Pitch and several others from the ruins. They had been trapped when the North Tower fell. Almost everyone else still inside the towers had died.

The dust from the World Trade Center ruins contained many **toxic** substances. Thousands of people who worked at Ground Zero later developed health problems.

The attacks affected the whole country. The **stock market**, theaters, and businesses closed. Sporting events were cancelled. For the first time, all American airports were shut down.

In New York, many families were missing loved ones. They checked hospitals to see if their relatives were there. They tried to remain hopeful.

Around the city, people posted information about missing relatives.

"I wasn't burnt or severely bruised. My pain was somewhere else—and it still is. Inside my heart, it hurts so hard."

—Roselyn Braud, the only person from the basement offices of the World Trade Center to survive

21

Hijackers

The planes that hit the World Trade Center were not the only ones that crashed on September 11. **Terrorists** had **hijacked** four planes that morning. Two hit the Twin Towers. Another hit military offices in the **Pentagon**. The last one crashed in a field in Pennsylvania. The United States was under attack.

Hijackers flew American Airlines Flight 77 into the Pentagon in Arlington, Virginia. It crashed through one section of the building.

Nineteen terrorists died when they crashed the planes on September 11. They were part of a terrorist group called **Al Qaeda**.

Osama bin Laden was the leader of Al Qaeda. He hoped to harm Americans and the American way of life. He had planned the attacks from his base in Afghanistan.

Osama bin Laden was wanted by police around the world.

About 2,800 people died in the World Trade Center attack. Another 184 innocent people were killed in the Pentagon attack. Forty passengers and crew members died in the crash in Pennsylvania.

America and the World

Around the world, people were horrified by the attacks against the United States. The leaders of Mexico, China, Great Britain, Egypt, and many other countries spoke out against the terrorists. They promised to support the United States.

Tony Blair, the British prime minister, called the attacks "terrible" and "shocking."

Americans were shocked, too. "We never believed that this could happen to us," said one college student in Minneapolis, Minnesota. "I feel very unsafe," said another college student after the attacks.

Many Americans also felt anger. Some wanted to fight the terrorists and anyone who supported them.

❝It was very scary in Ohio so it must have been very, very scary in New York.❞

—Erin, a fifth-grader from Ohio, writing to students in New York City

U.S. soldiers in Afghanistan

In October 2001, the United States went to war against the terrorists in Afghanistan. U.S. troops destroyed many of the training camps there and drove the terrorists into hiding.

America Recovers

Slowly, the country recovered. Airports and businesses opened again. The government created special airport **security** measures and passed laws to prevent future attacks.

Americans would never forget the people who died on 9/11. Families held funerals and **memorial services** for their loved ones. Police and firefighters cried as they buried friends and relatives. Newspapers printed pictures of the victims.

Six months after the attack, twin towers of light were beamed into the sky from Ground Zero to honor those who lost their lives.

At Ground Zero, designers have planned a special memorial. A museum will tell the stories of the victims and survivors of the attacks. Pools of water will show where the Twin Towers once stood. Everyone who visits will remember the tragedy and the heroes of September 11, 2001.

"We're going to rebuild, and we're going to be stronger than we were before . . . I want the people of New York to be an example to the rest of the country and the rest of the world that terrorism can't stop us."

–Rudolph Giuliani, mayor of New York City, September 11, 2001, speaking about the attacks

Many people were connected to the events of the 2001 World Trade Center attack. Here are four of them.

Commander Richard "Chief Pitch" Picciotto worked for the New York City Fire Department.

- Responded to an earlier disaster at the World Trade Center, in 1993, when terrorists set off a bomb in the garage
- Rushed to the Twin Towers on September 11 and began working to save people
- Ordered an evacuation of the North Tower after the South Tower collapsed
- Was trapped in the rubble when the North Tower fell, and was rescued by other firefighters

Omar Rivera worked on the 71st floor of the North Tower.

- Moved to the United States from Colombia
- At the time of the attack, had been blind for 15 years
- Refused to leave the World Trade Center without Salty, his guide dog who traveled to work with him every day
- Felt frightened for many weeks whenever he heard a siren or an airplane flying low

Osama bin Laden planned the World Trade Center attack.

- Was born to a wealthy family in Saudi Arabia and later inherited millions of dollars
- Used his money to train terrorists so that they could attack different countries
- Led Al Qaeda, the terrorist group that carried out the attacks of September 11, 2001
- Moved into caves in the mountains around the Afghan and Pakistani border to hide from American troops

Rudolph Giuliani was the mayor of New York City from 1994 to 2001.

- Urged New Yorkers to return to their normal lives after the attacks
- Attended funerals for many of the police officers and firefighters who died
- Gave speeches that inspired many Americans
- Won praise for his strength in dealing with the tragedy

Glossary

Al Qaeda (AHL KAY-duh)
a terrorist group that was responsible for the September 11th attacks on the United States

ash (ASH) a powdery substance that is left after something has been burned

collapsed (kuh-LAPST)
fell down or caved in

debris (duh-BREE) scattered pieces of something that has been destroyed

evacuation (i-*vak*-yoo-AY-shuhn)
the removal of people from a dangerous place

flammable (FLAM-uh-buhl)
able to catch fire easily

Ground Zero
(GROUND ZIHR-oh)
the place where the World Trade Center towers once stood

hijacked (HYE-jakt) illegally took control of an airplane or other vehicle by force

intercom (IN-tur-*kom*)
a speaker system that lets people communicate with those in another room

memorial services
(muh-MOR-ee-uhl SUR-viss-iz)
events that help people remember someone

Pentagon (PEN-tuh-gon)
the five-sided building in Virginia that serves as the headquarters of the U.S. Department of Defense

rubble (RUHB-uhl) broken pieces of rock, brick, or other materials

security (si-KYOOR-uh-tee)
safety

skyscraper (SKYE-*skray*-pur)
a very tall building

stock market (STOK MAR-kit)
a place where stocks and bonds are bought and sold

stories (STOR-eez) floors or levels of a building

survivors (sur-VYE-vurz)
people who have lived through a disaster

terrorists (TER-ur-ists)
people who use violence to get what they want

toxic (TOK-sik) poisonous, deadly

Bibliography

Lee, Nancy, Lonnie Schlein, and Mitchel Levitas, eds. *A Nation Challenged: A Visual History of 9/11 and Its Aftermath.* New York: The New York Times/Callaway (2002).

Picciotto, Richard, with Daniel Paisner. *Last Man Down: A Firefighter's Story of Survival and Escape from the World Trade Center.* New York: Berkley Books (2002).

www.cnn.com/SPECIALS/2001/trade.center/victim.accounts.html

www.september11news.com/

Read More

Britton, Tamara L. *The World Trade Center.* Edina, MN: Checkerboard Books (2002).

Lalley, Patrick. *9.11.01: Terrorists Attack the U.S.* Chicago, IL: Heinemann/Raintree (2002).

Wheeler, Jill C. *September 11, 2001: The Day That Changed America.* Edina, MN: ABDO & Daughters (2002).

Learn More Online

To learn more about the attack on the World Trade Center, visit
www.bearportpublishing.com/CodeRed

The Associated Press

The Associated Press

THE SUN rises
nesday, spotlights
inate the section of
Pentagon damaged
day by American
nes Flight 77. At left
e background is the
Capitol.

GHTERS IN New
City r the flag
and the of the
collapsed World Trade
Center towers Tuesday.

Index

About the Author

Jacqueline Dembar Greene is an award-winning author of more than 20 fiction and nonfiction books and stories, including *The Triangle Shirtwaist Factory Fire*. She has illustrated some of her nonfiction books with original photographs. Learn more at www.jdgbooks.com.